To

_____

From

_____

Date

_____

Anchored in Kindness

Who is Jesus?
A 30-Day Devotional Study

Thomas Bratton

Butterfly Books Publishing

Anchored in Kindness: Who is Jesus?
Copyright © Thomas Bratton 2025
Published in 2025 by Thomas Bratton in association with Butterfly Books
Publishing.
Butterfly Books Publishing is an independent publisher.

Cover Design by Butterfly Books Publishing
Interior Design by Butterfly Books Publishing
Edited and proofread by Katelyn Silva

Printed in the United States of America

ISBN-13 (paperback):978-1-965652-36-7
ISBN-13 (hardcover):

Unless otherwise indicated, all Scripture quotations are taken from the
Holy Bible, New Living Translation, copyright © 1996, 2004, 2015 by Tyndale
House Foundation. Used by permission of Tyndale House Publishers, Carol
Stream, Illinois 60188. All rights reserved.

Scripture quotations marked NIV are taken from the Holy Bible, New
International Version®, NIV®. Copyright 1973, 1978, 1984, 2011 by Biblica, Inc.
® Used by permission of Zondervan. All rights reserved worldwide.
www.Zondervan.com. The "NIV" and "New International Version" are
trademarks registered in the United States Patent and Trademark Office
by Biblica, Inc.® Scripture quotations marked NLV are from the New Life
Version. Copyright Christian Literature International. Scriptures marked
NKJV are taken from the New King James Version (NKJV)®. Copyright©
1982 by Thomas Nelson, Inc. Used by permission. All rights reserved.

Contents

Introduction 1

Day 1 5

Day 2 7

Day 3 8

Day 4 9

Day 5 10

Day 6 11

Day 7 12

Day 8 13

Day 9 14

Day 10 15

Day 11 16

Day 12 17

Day 13 18

Day 14 19

Day 15 20

Day 16 21

Day 17 22

Day 18 23

Day 19 24

Day 20 25

Day 21 26

Day 22 27

Day 23 28

Day 24 29

Day 25 30

Day 26 31

Day 27 32

Day 28 33

Day 29 34

Day 30 35

Additional Resources 37

Thank You! 38

Introduction

Today, people are becoming increasingly busier. Frequently burdened with obligations and a multitude of life's roles often leaves little time for relationships, a social life, even their own personal life or self-care. We are weighed down by so much on our shoulders that even being kind can seem difficult.

Amidst all of this business, I felt inspired to write a 30-day devotional: "Who is Jesus?"

We know Jesus is the Messiah, the Son of God, our savior. Yet I was encouraged to learn more about His character and His purpose. Why did Jesus come? Why did God send Him?

The truth is God loves us and wants to save us from our sins and this fallen world. Sometimes we are cruel and unkind, inconsistent with the temperament of Jesus.

A good friend of mine was telling me just last week about how a few people expressed their sarcasm towards her. Curious, I asked if she wanted to discuss this with me and how their rudeness made her feel. Though I know firsthand how unsolicited sly remarks feel, I wanted her to express her feelings. I couldn't help thinking, '*Where is Jesus amidst all this chaos of families and friends feeling it is okay to be disrespectful, rude, and unkind?'*

Jesus is Love

We all feel it among us. In Jesus' day, there was chaos among family and friends too. Jesus told Peter to turn the other cheek and be forgiving. And Paul said we are to make allowances for others. I felt empathetic with my friend. I've experienced similar situations throughout my life and have heard this from others as well. This kept bothering me knowing, "Love is kind, not rude, love is forgiving, not unjust, love is humble and not full of pride" (my version from 1 Corinthians 13).

This interaction also inspired me to craft 30 devotionals and Bible verses based upon love, kindness, and forgiveness which we can gather all throughout Scripture. Each heartfelt devotional with prayer is meant to be an encouragement for all of us to walk with Christ and share His love through our hearts and actions.

God is love. We love Him because He loves us. We're all created in God's image to show genuine affection with love for one another. Love your neighbor as yourself.

Forgiveness is for you as much as the other person who offends you so you will not become bitter. Remember, God chose to forgive you so you must forgive others.

Show kindness to everyone, be hospitable and helpful. Reach out and share the love of Jesus with thoughtfulness, respect, and admiration.

Remember, not everyone is the same. Just like the body is separate from the legs and the arms. They all function differently.

Blessing and Prayer

May God bless you and clothe you in love, kindness, humility, and may you use your gifts which have been freely bestowed upon you to bless others.
Pray with me:
Lord, we humbly ask you to soften our hearts and help us to show kindness to everyone, even when it is difficult. Help me rid myself of any resentments and forgive others as you have forgiven me. Holy Spirit, be my guide today and thereafter, that others would see your love through me, In Jesus name, amen.

Day 1

Noah waited another seven days and then released the dove again. This time it did not come back. Genesis 8:12

Have you been waiting on the Lord for something?

Many times, we must wait for the right time. I am sure you have heard the saying, "All in good time." Now I am telling you, "In God's time," as He expressed to Noah when it would be safe to depart the ark and be on dry land again.

Had Noah left the boat early and the flood waters not receded, everyone aboard may not have survived, but Noah learned to listen to God, just as he had when he built the ark despite being ridiculed by others. Noah preserved and took heart in trusting the Lord, listening, and meditating upon God's word.

Have patience and all good things will come to those who meditate upon the word of God in His time. Do not hurry, but like Noah, persevere.

Prayer

Lord, help me today to wait patiently for your perfect timing and to persevere through trials. Help me to trust you in whatever you've asked me to do, no matter the circumstances. I choose to follow your will. In Jesus' name, amen.

Day 2

For we are God's handiwork, created in Christ Jesus to do good works, which God prepared in advance for us to do. Ephesians 2:10

You are God's masterpiece. You have your own identity and abilities uniquely given to you by God. Think about that for a moment.

We are all different, possessing unique talents to help and encourage others, just like Christ has taught us.

Therefore, who can be against you when God is for you?

What skills do you have? How can you utilize them to help someone?

Prayer

Heavenly Father, thank you for making me unique and wonderful for your good plans and purpose! Help me today to walk according to your will, to use my gifts and abilities according to your plans, and to see the opportunities all around me to share your love.

Day 3

Jesus said unto them, "Blessed are those who have not seen and yet have believed." John 20:29

God orchestrated all events from the beginning of time. And He sent His one and only Son to advocate on our behalf, perform miracles, teach us how to live, suffer at the cross, and be resurrected before His ascension into Heaven. The purpose of the Bible is so that we will believe this truth and establish a relationship with Him.

We are called to read and meditate upon Scripture so we may have life in His name.

Consider a daily Bible reading plan and contemplate how that may apply to your life through prayer. Be Still and Listen.

Prayer

Heavenly Father, thank you for sending your Son Jesus to give His life for me so that I can have eternal life and an intimate relationship with you. Keep me focused on this beautiful truth that I may continually renew my mind and come boldly before the throne of grace. Amen.

Day 4

One who loves a pure heart and who speaks with grace will have the king for a friend. Proverbs 22:11

Communication is vital to everyone. How we convey our message is equally important as the message itself. Ever notice how some people have a form of elegance when speaking? They speak with confidence and make others feel comfortable.

Mary Angelou said, "People will forget what you said. People will forget what you did. But people will never forget how you made them feel."

Next time you have difficulty looking for the right words, pray that the Holy Spirit will speak through you so that you will not offend anyone and your words will be well-received and transformative.

Prayer

Lord, just as you promised that we need not worry what we will say concerning your words since we will receive the right words from the Holy Spirit, I ask that you lead me and put your words in my mouth. Let my words be gracious and seasoned with salt, abounding in love toward others. Amen.

Day 5

But because of his great love for us, God, who is rich in mercy, made us alive with Christ even when we were dead in transgressions—it is by grace you have been saved. Ephesians 2:4-5

There are similarities between mercy and grace, which are expressions of God's love for us. The difference: mercy is not getting what we deserve, and with grace we get what we don't deserve.

Many times in the Bible there are parables of God's mercy and grace. For example, Jesus told of the prodigal son who deserved to be chastised and given nothing, but instead his father celebrated richly when his son returned home. Through reading the Bible, you will inherently see the true differences in many other places as well, and you will also notice how God has extended the same mercy and grace unto you.

Prayer

Heavenly Father, thank you that you show me such mercy and grace by the precious gift of Jesus who was perfect in every way and yet took on my sins, taking the punishment I deserve, and giving me eternal life with you. Help me to lavish this same grace and mercy on others and lead them also to your gospel. Amen.

Day 6

May God, who gives this patience and encouragement, help you live in complete harmony with each other, as is fitting for followers of Christ Jesus. Romans 15:5

Scripture gives us hope and encouragement as we wait upon God's promises.

Teachers encourage their students to do well; guidance counselors encourage those who are seeking answers to many of life's situations.

Each one of us is called to encourage one another and build each other up. When we live in harmony, we are living in accordance with the way God intended us to live, each of us doing our part to help each other.

"What you're doing now is certainly helping someone, surely as someone sitting in the shade under a tree someone planted many years ago." - Warren Buffett

Prayer

Lord, help me to live in harmony with others around me. Help me not become too easily offended, but instead to show compassion with humility be a reflection of you toward others in Christ. Amen.

Day 7

Potiphar gave Joseph complete administrative responsibility over everything he owned. With Joseph there, he didn't worry about a thing. Genesis 39:6

God puts people in your life to help you, and blesses you so you may be a blessing to others.

Do you use your gifts to bless others? Several verses in Proverbs suggest seeking advice from the wise and the safety in seeking wise counsel. When you are blessed by others or receive Godly counsel from them, thank them for taking the time to help you. And thank God for sending those people your way.

Prayer

Take time to thank God for the wise people He has placed in your life and pray that God would continue to bless them also.

Day 8

So, then the Twelve called a meeting of all the believers. They said, "We apostles should spend our time teaching the word of God, not running a food program. Acts 6:2

The apostles knew the needs of others but could not do everything on their own. So they appointed others to help, and the community then was able to grow together, which brought unity to everyone.

We grow as a community by encouraging each other to assist in the service of others. In what ways does your community encourage each other to be of service?

Prayer

Lord Jesus, help me by the power of the Holy Spirit to see the needs of those around me and to have a heart of humility and readiness to serve. Help me to see when I can, and when I can't, and to encourage others to use their gifts for service also. Amen.

Day 9

Don't worry about anything; instead, pray about everything. Tell God what you need, and thank him for all he has done. Then you will experience God's peace, which exceeds anything we can understand. His peace will guard your hearts and minds as you live in Christ Jesus. Philippians 4:6-7

Each day we succumb to our daily lives and schedules, sometimes with great uncertainty.

Don't give in; instead, submit to God your schedule and your life and thank Him for leading you along the path that He has designed for you. Know that when things don't go according to *your* plan, they are going according to His. Trust Him.

When you get into harmony with God, you will soon experience true tranquility. Have you made your requests known to God and thanked Him for all He has done?

Prayer

Prayer: Heavenly Father, I have been worried about ...

I choose today to lay these things at your feet. I choose to trust your will and plan for my life. Help me walk according to your ways. Amen.

Day 10

If God is for us, who can ever be against us. Romans 8:31

Nothing can separate you from God's love. People pleasing will disappoint you at times; others may not even like you for whatever reason, and there may be nothing you can do to change that. They may spread rumors about you and even try to hurt you. It is more important to please God because His love will never fail, and He will protect you from evildoers.

Have you been nice to someone who is not nice to you?

Prayer

Take time to pray for them and ask God to remove any barriers that may keep you from loving them. Ask the Lord for discernment and wisdom in navigating different relationships and people and ask Him for courage to love them as Christ loves them. Ask God to give you the fear of the Lord and to walk in it.

Day 11

So now I am giving you a new commandment: Love each other. Just as I have loved you, you should love each other. John 13:34

Love is more than a word. It is a verb and requires action.

Jesus's example of love is unparalleled to anyone else or anything in existence.

We are called to aspire to the abundant examples of His great teachings.

How would you explain what real love is? Can you demonstrate love in your everyday life?

Prayer

Lord Jesus, what matchless love you have poured on me! Thank you for your perfect example of love. Help me to also love others as you have loved me. Amen.

Day 12

Always be humble and gentle. Be patient with each other, making allowance for each other's faults because of your love. Ephesians 4:2

When you look for your joy to come from others, you may be disappointed. It's better not to set your expectations too high and just enjoy the time you have with others. Learn from others. As Maya Angelou said, "They may not remember what you said, but they will remember how you made them feel."

Who can you make feel important today?

What can you do to make everyone feel important when in your presence?

Prayer

Lord, remind me that in you my joy is full and complete, and that my strength comes from your joy in me. Help me to be compassionate, forgiving, and patient with others around me. Work in me so others feel loved and uplifted when they are around me. Amen.

Day 13

For by the grace given me I say to every one of you: Do not think of yourself more highly than you ought, but rather think of yourself with sober judgment, in accordance with the faith God has distributed to each of you. Romans 12:3

We have each been given a gift of **"grace"** not to keep for ourselves but to share among each other.

Do you think you are better than someone else?

Extend to them the same grace the Lord has given to you, and make allowances for other people's faults since you do not know what they may be going through.

We all have our own story to tell. Be sure to share yours and also listen to someone else's story.

Prayer

Lord, help me to walk in true humility with a tender heart toward your people. Teach me to be quick to listen and slow to speak. Remind me of the depth of your grace and help me show it readily to others. Amen.

Day 14

The heart is deceitful above all things and beyond cure. Who can understand it? "I the Lord search the heart and examine the mind, to reward each person according to their conduct, according to what their deeds deserve." Jeremiah 17:9-10

Those who trust in God and have confidence in Him will be blessed according to His glorious riches. This is a promise from God.

He understands your motives, whether they are self-seeking or for the betterment of others.

Ask God to search your heart and remove any barriers that are not in alignment with God's will.

Prayer

Read Psalm 51 and pray it to the Lord over yourself.

Day 15

And let us not neglect our meeting together, as some people do, but encourage one another, especially now that the day of his return is drawing near. Hebrew 10:25

Gathering together is an important part of affirming your faith and hope, and a chance to encourage others and receive encouragement. Do not isolate yourself where you hinder the hope of someone in need of help.

Search for opportunities to do good works out of love for one another.

Small groups are a great opportunity to meet with others, encourage them, and share the good news that brings glory to our heavenly Father.

Prayer

Lord, thank you for the people you have put in my life and for the gifts you have given me. Help me to be attentive to others' needs as well and to use the gifts you've given me for your people and your glory. Amen.

Day 16

"I also tell you this: If two of you agree here on earth concerning anything you ask, my Father in heaven will do it for you. For where two or three who gather together as my followers, I am there among them."
Matthew 18:19-20

When we gather together as a community, Jesus moves among us and we help each other in times of devastation, those less fortunate, and satisfy the basic needs of each individual and family.

God prepares us in advance to do good works, which bring glory to the Father as He works all things for good for those who love Him.

Would you concur that "God is Good, All the Time"?

Prayer

Lord Jesus, thank you for your promise that you never leave us or forsake us and that you are in our midst when we gather together. As I gather with others, use me for the good works that bring you glory. Amen.

Day 17

Work willingly at whatever you do, as though you were working for the Lord rather than for people. Colossians 3:23

Many times, we do things that please people. And then there are times we fail miserably and disappoint others.

We succeed when we look to the Lord and serve Him through serving others. Sure, we still make mistakes, but we don't fail or disappoint Him either when we keep our eyes on Him.

Do you honor God with the gifts He has given you? Remember, you cannot serve two masters.

Prayer

Lord, please keep my eyes fixed on you. Help me to follow your lead, to serve as you served, and to obey you in the Holy Spirit which you have given. Reveal the gifts you've given to me, and help me to honor you with them. Amen.

Day 18

You can make many plans, but the Lord's purpose will prevail. Proverbs 19:21

God has great plans for you, plans to help you help others. Give careful consideration to your plans and seek the Lord's direction in everything you do.

Know your motives: God searches your heart and knows your true desires.

What are the true desires of your heart and the end result of them? Is it to gain more for yourself, or to build up others and God's kingdom? Keep your desires in harmony with God's plans for you and allow Him to lead you.

Prayer

Heavenly Father, I know that you are sovereign over all things and you have promised that you direct all my steps. Search my heart and cleanse me of any unrighteousness. Turn my heart toward you. Your will be done in me and through me. Amen.

Day 19

*Worry weighs a person down; an encouraging word
cheers a person up. Proverbs 12:25*

Sometimes you may need to say an encouraging
word to yourself.

One afternoon I thought that my lack of rest may
lead to my getting ill, but then I thought, '*Why worry
about that now? Therefore, enjoy the moment.*'

Repeat affirmations to yourself as well as to others.
Be fruitful with affirmations as they are stress
reducers for others as they are for you.

Practice affirmations of God's truth and promises
from His word.

Prompt

Make a list of these you can pray regularly.

Day 20

*Take delight in the Lord, and he will give you your
heart's desires. Psalms 37:4*

Just as when your children come to you, God loves
it when His children come to Him with their concerns,
and He also expects us to show gratitude towards Him
and all He has done for us.

When you make your requests known to God and
turn your free will over to Him, He will help you and
show you how to overcome any circumstance. He will
strengthen you and prepare you to do His work which
He has planned for you so that your soul may prosper.

How do you take delight in the Lord? Prayer,
meditating, and reading scripture are admirable ways
to show God you are interested in Him.

Remember, a relationship works both ways.

Prompt

Take time to just sit in the Lord's presence,
meditating on who He is or studying His word or just
worshipping Him.

Day 21

Instead, be kind to each other, tenderhearted, forgiving one another, just as God through Christ has forgiven you. Ephesians 4:32

The youth leader at our church said during one of his sermons, "It would not be a commandment if it were easy to love others." And he is right.

Therefore, we must make allowances for others and forgive them as we have been forgiven.

Are you looking into a mirror and seeing a reflection of yourself?

Search your heart. Is there someone you need to forgive?

Prayer

Heavenly Father, thank you for your great love, grace, mercy, and forgiveness. Show me who in my life against whom I am holding on to bitterness or unforgiveness. I choose now to forgive them and instead, to pray for them. Give me patience and grace toward this person. Amen.

Day 22

"You don't have enough faith," Jesus told them. "I tell you the truth, if you had faith even as small as a mustard seed, you could say to this mountain, 'Move from here to there,' and it would move. Nothing would be impossible." Matthew 17:20

Is seeing believing? Nothing is impossible if you believe, but we can't do it alone. We must have Faith that God is ultimately in control.

If we have faith and ask for something, it will be done according to the amount of faith we have.

What mountains has God already moved for you?

In what ways are your prayers too small?

Prayer

Lord, I thank you for the great and mighty work you have already done in my life. Please grant me the gift of your faith. Place your desires on my heart and grant me the boldness in my prayers. Amen.

Day 23

"The master said, 'Well done, my good and faithful servant. You have been faithful in handling this small amount, so now I will give you many more responsibilities. Let's celebrate together!'" Matthew 25:23

Once we have learned to be faithful with smaller tasks, then we will be entrusted with greater responsibility over more or larger tasks.

In what ways can you be faithful in what you currently have? Are there any commands the Lord has given you which you have yet to complete?

Have you been faithful to those who have shown their trust in you?

Do you desire for your responsibilities to be increased?

Prompt

Take time to pray over your current responsibilities and ask God to help you complete them and to grow in your faithfulness. Ask God to grant you greater responsibilities.

Day 24

But the Lord was with Joseph in the prison and showed him his faithful love. And the Lord made Joseph a favorite with the prison warden. Genesis 39:21

All throughout history, God has shown favor upon those who have been obedient.

Joseph endured many trials yet remained faithful to God. And in return, God showed favor upon him, giving him authority over everything the pharaoh owned.

Do you abide in the laws of God?

How has He shown favor upon the things you're in control of?

Prompt

Take time to thank Him for the blessings and favor He has already given you. Ask Him to help you to be obedient and faithful no matter your circumstances, and for His comfort and peace in trials.

Day 25

The disciples went and woke him up, shouting, "Master, Master, we're going to drown! When Jesus woke up, he rebuked the wind and the raging waves. Suddenly the storm stopped and all was calm. Then he asked them, "Where is your faith?" Luke 8:24-25

Faith is not always easy, but with God, all things are possible.

Does your life seem to be one storm after another? God is with you always and knows your pain.

Be steadfast and strong. Have faith and let God calm your storms.

Prompt

Take time now to cry out to the Lord. I encourage you to even journal through your current storm and submit it all to Him. Lay it at His feet, and then choose to remember works He has already done, prayers He has already answered, and choose to trust Him to carry you now.

Day 26

Then Peter came to him and asked, "Lord, how often should I forgive someone who sins against me? Seven times?"
"No, not seven times," Jesus replied, "But seventy times seven!" Matthew 18:21-22

Have you ever felt like you're going around that same mountain again, and again, and again?

Well, we, ourselves, want to be forgiven, but often we have not learned the lesson God is trying to teach us, and therefore we will not move forward with getting past a certain pattern or trial until that lesson is learned and we have repented.

Repentance is a change of direction, turning from your sins and toward God.

Prayer

Lord Jesus, help me to forgive often without holding bitterness or grudges. Help me to forgive as you forgave when you were on the cross. Amen.

Day 27

"Let the one who has never sinned throw the first stone!" John 8:7

Jesus did not come to earth to condemn us, but to save us from our sins, to show us the Father's love, and to have mercy on us.

Pardoning those who have made mistakes is having mercy on them, even when they don't deserve it.

Forgive them and they will see His example through you.

What example are you setting for others to see?

Prayer

Lord Jesus, thank you for your great love and forgiveness that you demonstrated even when you were on the cross. I pray that you would transform me from the inside out daily into your image so that through me, others see you. Use me to bring others into your flock. Amen.

Day 28

Do not let sin control the way you live; do not give in to sinful desires. Romans 6:12

Humans have many desires. Many times, we are tempted to follow the evil desires of the flesh instead of the righteous desires of the Holy Spirit. Ask God for His help to overcome any desire that is not pleasing to Him and to instead pursue the Godly desires He has placed within you.

Remember that, wherever your treasure is, there the desires of your heart will be. Luke 12:34.

Prompt

Take time to reflect on your desires. Pray over them and ask the Lord to reveal what He wants you to surrender to Him and what He wants you to pursue. Prayerfully ask Him to bring these desires to fruition through you.

Day 29

So, refuse to worry and keep your body healthy. But remember that youth, with a whole life before you, is meaningless. Ecclesiastes 11:10

Life is uncertain and should not be taken for granted.

"Worrying is like a rocking chair. It gives you something to do, but it doesn't get you anywhere." - Van Wilder.

Let go of worry today and every day. Instead, focus on what you're able to do today, even in this moment, and trust that God will guide your steps and work all for good.

Prayer

Heavenly Father, I have been worried about … (share your current worries, fears, and anxieties with Him). I choose to surrender these today. Help me to remember your word when I start to worry and to take all things to you instead. Strengthen me to focus on the steps and actions I can take instead of the things outside of my control. Amen.

Day 30

Seek the Kingdom of God above all else, and live righteously, and he will give you everything you need.
Matthew 6:33

God is faithful. He knows all your needs, and He will provide for those who love Him.

Submit yourself to God every day, and ask for His guidance. As you do this, He will open doors that no one else can open.

Take time to prayerfully seek God and ask Him what plans He has for you. Continue seeking and following as He leads with what He has given you, and watch as He paves the way before you.

Prompt

Write out a life plan that is in alignment with God's plans for you.

Becoming Anchored is a weekly devotional consisting of 52 devotionals of hope for strengthening your faith and trust in God. This devotional will guide you as you grow in your faith and personal relationship with the Lord, and ultimately help you become anchored in Him.

Life has many ups and downs and can often feel like you're attempting to navigate a raging storm at sea.

It's when we anchor ourselves in the Lord that we can experience peace through the storm, as when Jesus slept in the boat and was awakened by His disciples.

Continue your journey after this 30-day devotional by getting your copy here:

amazon.com/dp/B0BJ9B3ZTC.

ADDITIONAL RESOURCES

With the *Becoming Anchored* devotional, I also have a simple *Becoming Anchored Companion Journal* designed to help you dig deeper as you grow in hope, faith, and trust. Go to https://thomasbrattonauthor.com/becoming-anchored-gift to get your copy.

Follow me for updates concerning upcoming devotionals and other resources:

Follow me on Facebook:
https://www.facebook.com/3Pslivinnow

Follow me on Instagram:
https://www.instagram.com/thomas_bratton_author/

Follow me on LinkedIn:
https://www.linkedin.com/in/thomas-bratton-baab9244/

Follow me on Pinterest:
https://www.pinterest.com/becominganchoredtb/

Follow me on Goodreads:
https://www.goodreads.com/author/show/22971770.Thomas_Bratton

Visit my website and encouraging blog:
https://thomasbrattonauthor.com/

THANK YOU!

Thank you so much for taking the time to read *Anchored in Kindness: Who is Jesus?* I hope you found it immensely beneficial in your spiritual journey. Know as you go through life how precious you are to God, for He loves you.

I am grateful to all whom supported me and my endeavor during my writings, and to my writing coach, Katelyn Silva, for her enthusiasm and guidance. I would also like to thank my wife, Gina Bratton, for her love and encouragement to finish this devotional.

To my Mom and Dad who passed before I finished writing. It is through their values and love for family I adhere to a life of family, friends and service with the utmost integrity and love for God.

Would you take a moment and leave an honest review on the book page? It would mean so much to me and help get the devotional in the hands of others who would find it valuable.

.